Companion Playbook for

Weird & Wacky

Holiday Marketing Guide

I0025524

Award Winning Author/Designer

Ginger Marks

DocUmeant *Publishing*
244 5th Avenue
Suite G-200
NY, NY 10001
646-233-4366
www.DocUmeantPublishing.com

Weird & Wacky Holiday Marketing Guide Companion Playbook

Published by DocUmeant Publishing
244 5th Ave, Ste G–200
NY, NY 10001

646-233-4366

Layout & Design Ginger Marks
DocUmeant Designs

www.DocUmeantDesigns.com

ISBN 13: 978-1-937801-77-9

Contents

Introduction

This *Companion Playbook* is intended to help you to create, organize, and put the FUN back into your marketing plan. Each monthly calendar offers space for you to begin your planning.

Step 1: Refer to the Annual *Weird & Wacky Holiday Marketing Guide* for the complete list of holidays.

Step 2: Choose a holiday far enough ahead of the date to allow for proper preparation and planning.

Setp 3: In the *Companion Playbook* write in the chosen unusual holiday in the appropriate month/day space provided. Since each year the physical calendar days rotate, you will notice that the date numbers are left blank. This will enable you to make use of this *Companion Playbook* beginning today! I have included a perpetual calendar that you may find useful on the following page.

Step 4: As you discover tools and people who can assist you in your planning and implementation, quickly jot down the information either in the date area or the notes sections provided. To keep all your notes in one place you will find room for your notes in three places in this *Companion Playbook;*

1. the date area

2. the gray side note area

3. at the end of each month

On the subsequent page you will find a real life example of how to use this *Companion Playbook*. Thank you Wendy VanHatten for the wise suggestion of including it and doubly so for taking your time to provide this example.

Be sure to make use of the templates provided in the resource section of your *Weird & Wacky Holdiay Marketing Guide*. This will make your task of creating marketing tools easy. Do note, that no two years of the guide are exactly the same. Therefore, the holidays listed in some may or may not be listed in another, and the featured holidays and their subsequent resources will be unique to each edition. This makes for fun in collecting all past issues as you prepare your marketing plan.

Realize the Annual *Weird & Wacky Holiday Marketing Guide* is just that, a tool to use to jumpstart your imagination, while the *Companion Playbook* is used to organize and plan your marketing events.

If you need help designing your marketing pieces or tweaking the ones provided in the *Weird & Wacky Holiday Marketing Guide* send me a quick email at Ginger.Marks@DocUmeantDesigns.com and I'll be happy to assist you.

Here's to your marketing success!

Ginger Marks

PERPETUAL CALENDAR
1753 -2180

Locate the year—follow down the column to the month. The letter listed shows you which calendar letter is the correct calendar page.

			1753		1754		1755			1756			1757	
	1758		1759			1760			1761		1762		1763	
		1764			1765		1766		1767			1768		
	1769		1770		1771			1772			1773		1774	
	1775			1776			1777		1778		1779			1780
			1781		1782		1783			1784			1785	
	1786		1787			1788			1789		1790		1791	
		1792			1793		1794		1795			1796		
	1797		1798		1799		1800		1801		1802		1803	
		1804			1805		1806		1807			1808		
	1809		1810		1811			1812			1813		1814	
	1815			1816			1817		1818		1819			1820
			1821		1822		1823			1824			1825	
	1826		1827			1828			1829		1830		1831	
		1832			1833		1834		1835			1836		
	1837		1838		1839			1840			1841		1842	
	1843			1844			1845		1846		1847			1848
			1849		1850		1851			1852			1853	
	1854		1855			1856			1857		1858		1859	
		1860			1861		1862		1863			1864		
	1865		1866		1867			1868			1869		1870	
	1871			1872			1873		1874		1875			1876
			1877		1878		1879			1880			1881	
	1882		1883			1884			1885		1886		1887	
		1888			1889		1890		1891			1892		
	1893		1894		1895			1896			1897		1898	
	1899		1900		1901		1902		1903			1904		
	1905		1906		1907			1908			1909		1910	
	1911			1912			1913		1914		1915			1916
			1917		1918		1919			1920			1921	
	1922		1923			1924			1925		1926		1927	
		1928			1929		1930		1931			1932		
	1933		1934		1935			1936			1937		1938	
	1939			1940			1941		1942		1943			1944
			1945		1946		1947			1948			1949	
	1950		1951			1952			1953		1954		1955	
		1956			1957		1958		1959			1960		
	1961		1962		1963			1964			1965		1966	
January	A31	A31	B31	B31	C31	C31	D31	D31	E31	E31	F31	F31	G31	G31
February	D28	D29	E28	E29	F28	F29	G28	G29	A28	A29	B28	B29	C28	C29
March	D31	E31	E31	F31	F31	G31	G31	A31	A31	B31	B31	C31	C31	D31
April	G30	A30	A30	B30	B30	C30	C30	D30	D30	E30	E30	F30	F30	G30
May	B31	C31	C31	D31	D31	E31	E31	F31	F31	G31	G31	A31	A31	B31
June	E30	F30	F30	G30	G30	A30	A30	B30	B30	C30	C30	D30	D30	E30
July	G31	A31	A31	B31	B31	C31	C31	D31	D31	E31	E31	F31	F31	G31
August	C31	D31	D31	E31	E31	F31	F31	G31	G31	A31	A31	B31	B31	C31
September	F30	G30	G30	A30	A30	B30	B30	C30	C30	D30	D30	E30	E30	F30
October	A31	B31	B31	C31	C31	D31	D31	E31	E31	F31	F31	G31	G31	A31
November	D30	E30	E30	F30	F30	G30	G30	A30	A30	B30	B30	C30	C30	D30
December	F31	G31	G31	A31	A31	B31	B31	C31	C31	D31	D31	E31	E31	F31

1967			1968			1969		1970		1971			1972	
		1973		1974		1975			1976			1977		
1978		1979			1980			1981		1982		1983		
	1984			1985		1986		1987			1988			
1989		1990		1991			1992			1993		1994		
1995			1996			1997		1998		1999			2000	
		2001		2002		2003			2004			2005		
2006		2007			2008			2009		2010		2011		
	2012			2013		2014		2015			2016			
2017		2018		2019			2020			2021		2022		
2023			2024			2025		2026		2027			2028	
		2029		2030		2031			2032			2033		
2034		2035			2036			2037		2038		2039		
	2040			2041		2042		2043			2044			
2045		2046		2047			2048			2049		2050		
2051			2052			2053		2054		2055			2056	
		2057		2058		2059			2060			2061		
2062		2063			2064			2065		2066		2067		
	2068			2069		2070		2071			2072			
2073		2074		2075			2076			2077		2078		
2079			2080			2081		2082		2083			2084	
		2085		2086		2087			2088			2089		
2090		2091			2092			2093		2094		2095		
	2096			2097		2098		2099		2100		2101		
2102		2103			2104			2105		2106		2107		
	2108			2109		2110		2111			2112			
2113		2114		2115			2116			2117		2118		
2119			2120			2121		2122		2123			2124	
		2125		2126		2127			2128			2129		
2130		2131			2132			2133		2134		2135		
	2136			2137		2138		2139			2140			
2141		2142		2143			2144			2145		2146		
2147			2148			2149		2150		2151			2152	
		2153		2154		2155			2156			2157		
2158		2159			2160			2161		2162		2163		
	2164			2165		2166		2167			2168			
2169		2170		2171			2172			2173		2174		
2175			2176			2177		2178		2179			2180	
A31	A31	B31	B31	C31	C31	D31	D31	E31	E31	F31	F31	G31	G31	January
D28	D29	E28	E29	F28	F29	G28	G29	A28	A29	B28	B29	C28	C29	February
D31	E31	E31	F31	F31	G31	G31	A31	A31	B31	B31	C31	C31	D31	March
G30	A30	A30	B30	B30	C30	C30	D30	D30	E30	E30	F30	F30	G30	April
B31	C31	C31	D31	D31	E31	E31	F31	F31	G31	G31	A31	A31	B31	May
E30	F30	F30	G30	G30	A30	A30	B30	B30	C30	C30	D30	D30	E30	June
G31	A31	A31	B31	B31	C31	C31	D31	D31	E31	E31	F31	F31	G31	July
C31	D31	D31	E31	E31	F31	F31	G31	G31	A31	A31	B31	B31	C31	August
F30	G30	G30	A30	A30	B30	B30	C30	C30	D30	D30	E30	E30	F30	September
A31	B31	B31	C31	C31	D31	D31	E31	E31	F31	F31	G31	G31	A31	October
D30	E30	E30	F30	F30	G30	G30	A30	A30	B30	B30	C30	C30	D30	November
F31	G31	G31	A31	A31	B31	B31	C31	C31	D31	D31	E31	E31	F31	December

A

Su	Mo	Tu	We	Th	Fr	Sa
01	02	03	04	05	06	07
08	09	10	11	12	13	14
15	16	17	18	19	20	21
22	23	24	25	26	27	28
29	30	31				

B

Su	Mo	Tu	We	Th	Fr	Sa
	01	02	03	04	05	06
07	08	09	10	11	12	13
14	15	16	17	18	19	20
21	22	23	24	25	26	27
28	29	30	31			

C

Su	Mo	Tu	We	Th	Fr	Sa
		01	02	03	04	05
06	07	08	09	10	11	12
13	14	15	16	17	18	19
20	21	22	23	24	25	26
27	28	29	30	31		

D

Su	Mo	Tu	We	Th	Fr	Sa
			01	02	03	04
05	06	07	08	09	10	11
12	13	14	15	16	17	18
19	20	21	22	23	24	25
26	27	28	29	30	31	

E

Su	Mo	Tu	We	Th	Fr	Sa
				01	02	03
04	05	06	07	08	09	10
11	12	13	14	15	16	17
18	19	20	21	22	23	24
25	26	27	28	29	30	31

F

Su	Mo	Tu	We	Th	Fr	Sa
					01	02
03	04	05	06	07	08	09
10	11	12	13	14	15	16
17	18	19	20	21	22	23
24	25	26	27	28	29	30
31						

G

Su	Mo	Tu	We	Th	Fr	Sa
						01
02	03	04	05	06	07	08
09	10	11	12	13	14	15
16	17	18	19	20	21	22
23	24	25	26	27	28	29
30	31					

EXAMPLE

Weird & Wacky Holiday Marketing Calendar

JANUARY

Use this notes area to list points of interest, e.g., committee members, designers/illustrators, supporters/donors, consultants, printers, venues.

Prepare for Speech about National Nothing Day

Incorporate writing or not writing on this day.

Talk about Writer's block & writing nothing.

Make Door Prize — use idea in Appendix Ask audience to write nothing. Whoever writes the word 'nothing' wins.

Monday 16

National Nothing Day
 use in a speech to a writers' group
 Give Door Prize — offer a contest

Tuesday

Wednesday

Thursday

Friday

Saturday

Sunday

Fact:

Inspiration
will come if it
finds you working.

Use this notes area to list points of interest, e.g., committee members, designers/illustrators, supporters/donors, consultants, printers, venues.

Monday

Tuesday

Wednesday

Thursday

Friday

Saturday

Sunday

Monday

Tuesday

Wednesday

Thursday

Friday

Saturday

Sunday

Use this notes area to list points of interest, e.g., committee members, designers/illustrators, supporters/donors, consultants, printers, venues.

Weird & Wacky Holiday Marketing Calendar

JANUARY

Use this notes area to list points of interest, e.g., committee members, designers/illustrators, supporters/donors, consultants, printers, venues.

Monday

Tuesday

Wednesday

Thursday

Friday

Saturday

Sunday

Monday

Tuesday

Wednesday

Thursday

Friday

Saturday   **Sunday**

Use this notes area to list points of interest, e.g., committee members, designers/illustrators, supporters/donors, consultants, printers, venues.

Weird & Wacky Holiday Marketing Calendar

JANUARY

Use this notes area to list points of interest, e.g., committee members, designers/illustrators, supporters/donors, consultants, printers, venues.

Monday

Tuesday

Wednesday

Thursday

Friday

Saturday

Sunday

Monday

Tuesday

Wednesday

Thursday

Friday

Saturday   **Sunday**

Use this notes area to list points of interest, e.g., committee members, designers/illustrators, supporters/donors, consultants, printers, venues.

JANUARY NOTES:

JANUARY NOTES:

JANUARY NOTES:

Social Media Fact:

23% of Facebook users check their account more than 5 times a day.

Weird & Wacky Holiday Marketing Calendar

FEBUARY

Use this notes area to list points of interest, e.g., committee members, designers/illustrators, supporters/donors, consultants, printers, venues.

Monday

Tuesday

Wednesday

Thursday

Friday

Saturday

Sunday

Monday

Tuesday

Wednesday

Thursday

Friday

Saturday   **Sunday**

Use this notes area to list points of interest, e.g., committee members, designers/illustrators, supporters/donors, consultants, printers, venues.

Weird & Wacky Holiday Marketing Calendar

FEBUARY

Use this notes area to list points of interest, e.g., committee members, designers/illustrators, supporters/donors, consultants, printers, venues.

Monday

Tuesday

Wednesday

Thursday

Friday

Saturday

Sunday

Monday

Tuesday

Wednesday

Thursday

Friday

Saturday   **Sunday**

Use this notes area to list points of interest, e.g., committee members, designers/illustrators, supporters/donors, consultants, printers, venues.

Weird & Wacky Holiday Marketing Calendar

FEBUARY

Use this notes area to list points of interest, e.g., committee members, designers/illustrators, supporters/donors, consultants, printers, venues.

Monday

Tuesday

Wednesday

Thursday

Friday

Saturday

Sunday

Monday

Tuesday

Wednesday

Thursday

Friday

Saturday   **Sunday**

Use this notes area to list points of interest, e.g., committee members, designers/illustrators, supporters/donors, consultants, printers, venues.

FEBRUARY NOTES:

FEBRUARY NOTES:

FEBRUARY NOTES:

Social Media Fact:
75%
of consumers are
highly likely to
delete emails they
can't read on their
smartphone.

Weird & Wacky Holiday Marketing Calendar

MARCH

Use this notes area to list points of interest, e.g., committee members, designers/illustrators, supporters/donors, consultants, printers, venues.

Monday

Tuesday

Wednesday

Thursday

Friday

Saturday

Sunday

Monday

Tuesday

Wednesday

Thursday

Friday

Saturday   **Sunday**

Use this notes area to list points of interest, e.g., committee members, designers/illustrators, supporters/donors, consultants, printers, venues.

Weird & Wacky Holiday Marketing Calendar

MARCH

Use this notes area to list points of interest, e.g., committee members, designers/illustrators, supporters/donors, consultants, printers, venues.

Monday

Tuesday

Wednesday

Thursday

Friday

Saturday

Sunday

Monday

Tuesday

Wednesday

Thursday

Friday

Saturday   **Sunday**

Use this notes area to list points of interest, e.g., committee members, designers/illustrators, supporters/donors, consultants, printers, venues.

Weird & Wacky Holiday Marketing Calendar

MARCH

Use this notes area to list points of interest, e.g., committee members, designers/illustrators, supporters/donors, consultants, printers, venues.

Monday

Tuesday

Wednesday

Thursday

Friday

Saturday

Sunday

Monday

Tuesday

Wednesday

Thursday

Friday

Saturday   **Sunday**

Use this notes area to list points of interest, e.g., committee members, designers/illustrators, supporters/donors, consultants, printers, venues.

MARCH NOTES:

MARCH NOTES:

MARCH NOTES:

Social Media Fact:
55%
of consumers share
their purchases
socially on Facebook,
Twitter, Pintrest and
other social sites.

Weird & Wacky Holiday Marketing Calendar

APRIL

Use this notes area to list points of interest, e.g., committee members, designers/illustrators, supporters/donors, consultants, printers, venues.

Monday

Tuesday

Wednesday

Thursday

Friday

Saturday

Sunday

Monday

Tuesday

Wednesday

Thursday

Friday

Saturday   **Sunday**

Use this notes area to list points of interest, e.g., committee members, designers/illustrators, supporters/donors, consultants, printers, venues.

Weird & Wacky Holiday Marketing Calendar

APRIL

Use this notes area to list points of interest, e.g., committee members, designers/illustrators, supporters/donors, consultants, printers, venues.

Monday

Tuesday

Wednesday

Thursday

Friday

Saturday

Sunday

Monday

Tuesday

Wednesday

Thursday

Friday

Saturday   **Sunday**

Use this notes area to list points of interest, e.g., committee members, designers/illustrators, supporters/donors, consultants, printers, venues.

Weird & Wacky Holiday Marketing Calendar

APRIL

Use this notes area to list points of interest, e.g., committee members, designers/illustrators, supporters/donors, consultants, printers, venues.

Monday

Tuesday

Wednesday

Thursday

Friday

Saturday

Sunday

Monday

Tuesday

Wednesday

Thursday

Friday

Saturday

Sunday

Use this notes area to list points of interest, e.g., committee members, designers/illustrators, supporters/donors, consultants, printers, venues.

APRIL NOTES:

APRIL NOTES:

APRIL NOTES:

Social Media Fact:
72%
of consumers trust
online reviews as
much as personal
recommendations.

Weird & Wacky Holiday Marketing Calendar

MAY

Use this notes area to list points of interest, e.g., committee members, designers/illustrators, supporters/donors, consultants, printers, venues.

Monday

Tuesday

Wednesday

Thursday

Friday

Saturday

Sunday

Monday

Tuesday

Wednesday

Thursday

Friday

Saturday

Sunday

Weird & Wacky Holiday Marketing Calendar

MAY

Use this notes area to list points of interest, e.g., committee members, designers/illustrators, supporters/donors, consultants, printers, venues.

Weird & Wacky Holiday Marketing Calendar

MAY

Use this notes area to list points of interest, e.g., committee members, designers/illustrators, supporters/donors, consultants, printers, venues.

Monday

Tuesday

Wednesday

Thursday

Friday

Saturday

Sunday

Monday

Tuesday

Wednesday

Thursday

Friday

Saturday

Sunday

Use this notes area to list points of interest, e.g., committee members, designers/illustrators, supporters/donors, consultants, printers, venues.

Weird & Wacky Holiday Marketing Calendar

MAY

Use this notes area to list points of interest, e.g., committee members, designers/illustrators, supporters/donors, consultants, printers, venues.

Monday

Tuesday

Wednesday

Thursday

Friday

Saturday

Sunday

Monday

Tuesday

Wednesday

Thursday

Friday

Saturday

Sunday

Use this notes area to list points of interest, e.g., committee members, designers/illustrators, supporters/donors, consultants, printers, venues.

MAY NOTES:

MAY NOTES:

MAY NOTES:

Social Media Fact:

Companies with an active blog generate 67% more leads per month!

Weird & Wacky Holiday Marketing Calendar

JUNE

Use this notes area to list points of interest, e.g., committee members, designers/illustrators, supporters/donors, consultants, printers, venues.

Monday

Tuesday

Wednesday

Thursday

Friday

Saturday

Sunday

Monday

Tuesday

Wednesday

Thursday

Friday

Saturday   **Sunday**

Use this notes area to list points of interest, e.g., committee members, designers/illustrators, supporters/donors, consultants, printers, venues.

Weird & Wacky Holiday Marketing Calendar

JUNE

Use this notes area to list points of interest, e.g., committee members, designers/illustrators, supporters/donors, consultants, printers, venues.

Monday

Tuesday

Wednesday

Thursday

Friday

Saturday

Sunday

Monday

Tuesday

Wednesday

Thursday

Friday

Saturday

Sunday

Use this notes area to list points of interest, e.g., committee members, designers/illustrators, supporters/donors, consultants, printers, venues.

Weird & Wacky Holiday Marketing Calendar

JUNE

Use this notes area to list points of interest, e.g., committee members, designers/illustrators, supporters/donors, consultants, printers, venues.

Monday

Tuesday

Wednesday

Thursday

Friday

Saturday

Sunday

Monday

Tuesday

Wednesday

Thursday

Friday

Saturday

Sunday

Use this notes area to list points of interest, e.g., committee members, designers/illustrators, supporters/donors, consultants, printers, venues.

JUNE NOTES:

JUNE NOTES:

JUNE NOTES:

Social Media Fact:

6 _billion_ hours of videos are watched every month on YouTube!

Weird & Wacky Holiday Marketing Calendar

JULY

Use this notes area to list points of interest, e.g., committee members, designers/illustrators, supporters/donors, consultants, printers, venues.

Monday

Tuesday

Wednesday

Thursday

Friday

Saturday

Sunday

Monday

Tuesday

Wednesday

Thursday

Friday

Saturday

Sunday

Use this notes area to list points of interest, e.g., committee members, designers/illustrators, supporters/donors, consultants, printers, venues.

Weird & Wacky Holiday Marketing Calendar

JULY

Use this notes area to list points of interest, e.g., committee members, designers/illustrators, supporters/donors, consultants, printers, venues.

Monday

Tuesday

Wednesday

Thursday

Friday

Saturday

Sunday

Monday

Tuesday

Wednesday

Thursday

Friday

Saturday   **Sunday**

Use this notes area to list points of interest, e.g., committee members, designers/illustrators, supporters/donors, consultants, printers, venues.

Weird & Wacky Holiday Marketing Calendar

JULY

Use this notes area to list points of interest, e.g., committee members, designers/illustrators, supporters/donors, consultants, printers, venues.

Monday

Tuesday

Wednesday

Thursday

Friday

Saturday

Sunday

Monday

Tuesday

Wednesday

Thursday

Friday

Saturday

Sunday

Use this notes area to list points of interest, e.g., committee members, designers/illustrators, supporters/donors, consultants, printers, venues.

JULY NOTES:

JULY NOTES:

JULY NOTES:

Marketing Fact:

Marketing can be
FUN!
...and when it's FUN,
It's EASY and
PROFITABLE too!

Weird & Wacky Holiday Marketing Calendar

AUGUST

Use this notes area to list points of interest, e.g., committee members, designers/illustrators, supporters/donors, consultants, printers, venues.

Monday

Tuesday

Wednesday

Thursday

Friday

Saturday

Sunday

Monday

Tuesday

Wednesday

Thursday

Friday

Saturday

Sunday

Use this notes area to list points of interest, e.g., committee members, designers/illustrators, supporters/donors, consultants, printers, venues.

Weird & Wacky Holiday Marketing Calendar

AUGUST

Use this notes area to list points of interest, e.g., committee members, designers/illustrators, supporters/donors, consultants, printers, venues.

Monday

Tuesday

Wednesday

Thursday

Friday

Saturday

Sunday

Monday

Tuesday

Wednesday

Thursday

Friday

Saturday

Sunday

Use this notes area to list points of interest, e.g., committee members, designers/illustrators, supporters/donors, consultants, printers, venues.

Weird & Wacky Holiday Marketing Calendar

AUGUST

Use this notes area to list points of interest, e.g., committee members, designers/illustrators, supporters/donors, consultants, printers, venues.

Monday

Tuesday

Wednesday

Thursday

Friday

Saturday

Sunday

Monday

Tuesday

Wednesday

Thursday

Friday

Saturday

Sunday

Use this notes area to list points of interest, e.g., committee members, designers/illustrators, supporters/donors, consultants, printers, venues.

AUGUST NOTES:

AUGUST NOTES:

AUGUST NOTES:

Marketing Fact:
55%
of consumers have
scanned a QR code.
18%
have purchased
after that.

Weird & Wacky Holiday Marketing Calendar

SEPTEMBER

Use this notes area to list points of interest, e.g., committee members, designers/illustrators, supporters/donors, consultants, printers, venues.

Monday

Tuesday

Wednesday

Thursday

Friday

Saturday

Sunday

Monday

Tuesday

Wednesday

Thursday

Friday

Saturday

Sunday

Use this notes area to list points of interest, e.g., committee members, designers/illustrators, supporters/donors, consultants, printers, venues.

Weird & Wacky Holiday Marketing Calendar

SEPTEMBER

Use this notes area to list points of interest, e.g., committee members, designers/illustrators, supporters/donors, consultants, printers, venues.

Monday

Tuesday

Wednesday

Thursday

Friday

Saturday

Sunday

Monday

Tuesday

Wednesday

Thursday

Friday

Saturday

Sunday

Use this notes area to list points of interest, e.g., committee members, designers/illustrators, supporters/donors, consultants, printers, venues.

Weird & Wacky Holiday Marketing Calendar

SEPTEMBER

Use this notes area to list points of interest, e.g., committee members, designers/illustrators, supporters/donors, consultants, printers, venues.

Monday

Tuesday

Wednesday

Thursday

Friday

Saturday

Sunday

Monday

Tuesday

Wednesday

Thursday

Friday

Saturday

Sunday

Use this notes area to list points of interest, e.g., committee members, designers/illustrators, supporters/donors, consultants, printers, venues.

SEPTEMBER NOTES:

SEPTEMBER NOTES:

SEPTEMBER NOTES:

Social Media Fact:
Over 34%
of marketers use
Twitter
to successfully
generate leads.

Weird & Wacky Holiday Marketing Calendar

OCTOBER

Use this notes area to list points of interest, e.g., committee members, designers/illustrators, supporters/donors, consultants, printers, venues.

Monday

Tuesday

Wednesday

Thursday

Friday

Saturday

Sunday

Monday

Tuesday

Wednesday

Thursday

Friday

Saturday

Sunday

Use this notes area to list points of interest, e.g., committee members, designers/illustrators, supporters/donors, consultants, printers, venues.

Use this notes area to list points of interest, e.g., committee members, designers/illustrators, supporters/donors, consultants, printers, venues.

Monday

Tuesday

Wednesday

Thursday

Friday

Saturday

Sunday

Monday

Tuesday

Wednesday

Thursday

Friday

Saturday

Sunday

Use this notes area to list points of interest, e.g., committee members, designers/illustrators, supporters/donors, consultants, printers, venues.

Weird & Wacky Holiday Marketing Calendar

OCTOBER

Use this notes area to list points of interest, e.g., committee members, designers/illustrators, supporters/donors, consultants, printers, venues.

Monday

Tuesday

Wednesday

Thursday

Friday

Saturday

Sunday

Monday

Tuesday

Wednesday

Thursday

Friday

Saturday

Sunday

Use this notes area to list points of interest, e.g., committee members, designers/illustrators, supporters/donors, consultants, printers, venues.

www.HolidayMarketingGuide.com

OCTOBER NOTES:

OCTOBER NOTES:

OCTOBER NOTES:

Marketing Fact:

9 out of 10 mobile searches lead to action.
Over half lead to purchase.

Weird & Wacky Holiday Marketing Calendar

NOVEMBER

Use this notes area to list points of interest, e.g., committee members, designers/illustrators, supporters/donors, consultants, printers, venues.

Monday

Tuesday

Wednesday

Thursday

Friday

Saturday

Sunday

Monday

Tuesday

Wednesday

Thursday

Friday

Saturday

Sunday

Use this notes area to list points of interest, e.g., committee members, designers/illustrators, supporters/donors, consultants, printers, venues.

Use this notes area to list points of interest, e.g., committee members, designers/illustrators, supporters/donors, consultants, printers, venues.

Monday

Tuesday

Wednesday

Thursday

Friday

Saturday

Sunday

Monday

Tuesday

Wednesday

Thursday

Friday

Saturday

Sunday

Use this notes area to list points of interest, e.g., committee members, designers/illustrators, supporters/donors, consultants, printers, venues.

Weird & Wacky Holiday Marketing Calendar

NOVEMBER

Use this notes area to list points of interest, e.g., committee members, designers/illustrators, supporters/donors, consultants, printers, venues.

Monday

Tuesday

Wednesday

Thursday

Friday

Saturday

Sunday

Monday

Tuesday

Wednesday

Thursday

Friday

Saturday

Sunday

Use this notes area to list points of interest, e.g., committee members, designers/illustrators, supporters/donors, consultants, printers, venues.

NOVEMBER NOTES:

NOVEMBER NOTES:

NOVEMBER NOTES:

Marketing Fact:
60%
of people say they
open an email
based on the
subject line.

Weird & Wacky Holiday Marketing Calendar

DECEMBER

Use this notes area to list points of interest, e.g., committee members, designers/illustrators, supporters/donors, consultants, printers, venues.

Monday

Tuesday

Wednesday

Thursday

Friday

Saturday

Sunday

Monday

Tuesday

Wednesday

Thursday

Friday

Saturday

Sunday

Use this notes area to list points of interest, e.g., committee members, designers/illustrators, supporters/donors, consultants, printers, venues.

Weird & Wacky Holiday Marketing Calendar

DECEMBER

Use this notes area to list points of interest, e.g., committee members, designers/illustrators, supporters/donors, consultants, printers, venues.

Monday

Tuesday

Wednesday

Thursday

Friday

Saturday

Sunday

Monday

Tuesday

Wednesday

Thursday

Friday

Saturday

Sunday

Use this notes area to list points of interest, e.g., committee members, designers/illustrators, supporters/donors, consultants, printers, venues.

Weird & Wacky Holiday Marketing Calendar

DECEMBER

Use this notes area to list points of interest, e.g., committee members, designers/illustrators, supporters/donors, consultants, printers, venues.

Monday

Tuesday

Wednesday

Thursday

Friday

Saturday

Sunday

Monday

Tuesday

Wednesday

Thursday

Friday

Saturday

Sunday

Use this notes area to list points of interest, e.g., committee members, designers/illustrators, supporters/donors, consultants, printers, venues.

DECEMBER NOTES:

DECEMBER NOTES:

DECEMBER NOTES:

Since the *Weird & Wacky Holiday Marketing Guide* has been available, it has won awards year-after-year, and been steadily in the top #1 or #2 Best-Seller lists in the Business Marketing category on America's biggest retailer.

With the addition of this *Companion Playbook,* you now have a tool at your fingertips that will make your marketing efforts easy to plan, prepare, and implement.

I would love to hear from you how you have used these tools (admin@holidaymarketingguide.com) and remind you to visit http://www.HolidayMarketingGuide.com often to get the FREE BONUS *Weird & Wacky Holiday Marketing* IDEA provided to you each and every month.

Here's to a fun and prosperous year,

Ginger Markes

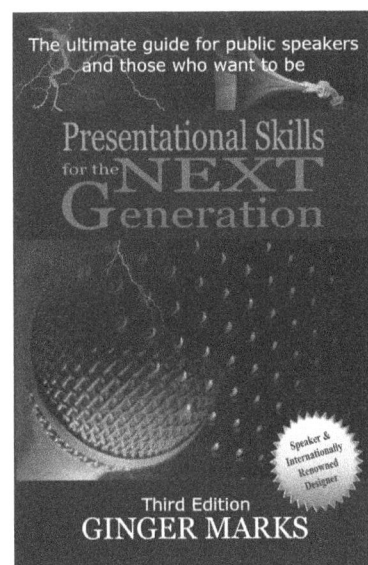

www.ingramcontent.com/pod-product-compliance
Lightning Source LLC
Chambersburg PA
CBHW080051280326

41934CB00014B/3281